KIDS' DIVORCE WORKBOOK - Revised

A Practical Guide That Helps Kids Understand
DIVORCE HAPPENS TO THE NICEST KIDS

A book by, for, and about kids
with
Michael S. Prokop, M.Ed., Consulting Psychologist

**Illustrated by Hannah, Audrey, Mikee,
and Dennis J. McCullough**

Kaya Books ©   Alegra House Publishers

KIDS' DIVORCE WORKBOOK - Revised

Michael S. Prokop, M. Ed.
Consulting Psychologist

Alegra House Publishers
Post Office Box 1443
Warren, Ohio 44482 U.S.A.

Copyright © 1986, Revised Edition© 2001 by Michael S. Prokop

ISBN 0-933879-42-3

2nd Printing	1988
3rd Printing	1993
4th Printing	2001

This book belongs to

_____ ,

a nice kid.

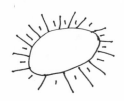

A Note to the Reader

This book is designed to help children understand divorce and themselves. It is sold with the understanding that the publisher and author are not engaged in rendering legal or professional services. If legal or professional services are required, a competent professional should be sought.

Table of Contents

Dear Kids,

This is a fun workbook that will help you better understand your parents' divorce and ideas in the book called *Divorce Happens to the Nicest Kids.*

This is your workbook which includes drawing, coloring, and writing activities. As you complete the activities, you will discover many things about yourself and divorce.

These "discoveries" will help you see that you are a nice person who can cope with your parents' divorce. Then you will understand why people often say that divorce happens to the nicest kids!

Be sure to ask for help if you have any questions. Have fun, learn, and enjoy the book!

Michael S. Prokop

Michael S. Prokop
Consulting Psychologist

Divorce happens to over one million nice kids each year.

Chapter 1

Understanding Yourself - You Are A Nice Person

All kids are nice human beings. Write down three nice things about yourself.

    1.

    2.

    3.

Happiness is a feeling of joy and well being. Name three things that make you happy.

    1.

    2.

    3.

Even though my parents are divorced,
I'm still a nice kid.

I help my mom.

All nice kids, including you, can be happy. Draw a picture of yourself smiling.

Participating in activities and doing things helps kids feel good about themselves. Write down three things you like to do.

1.

2.

3.

All kids have strengths and do certain things well. Write down three things you can do well.

1.

2.

3.

When kids help others they help themselves.

Nice things happen to kids everyday. These things may include seeing a sunset, playing with a friend, or eating a hamburger. Write three nice things that happened to you today.

1.

2.

3.

All kids have special things they like to do. Doing special things helps kids feel important. Write down three special things you like to do at school or home.

1.

2.

3.

Draw a picture of yourself doing something you can do well.

All kids have someone they admire, like, or look up to.
Draw a picture of your best friend or favorite person.

Playing and talking with friends help kids relax.

Kids learn to be happy even though their parents are divorced.

Chapter 2

Understanding Divorce and Families

Paying compliments or saying nice things to people helps kids feel better. It also helps others feel good about themselves. Write three nice things you could say to a friend.

1.

2.

3.

Think about kids in your neighborhood and at school; some of them also have divorced parents. Write the names of kids with divorced parents.

1.

2.

3.

A divorce is when your parents decide they no longer want to be married. They are not happy living together and decide to stop being husband and wife. They will still be your parents.

Three of my fRiends
have divoRced Parents.

Matching. Place the letter of each word in front of its definition. Answers on next page.

a. divorce   b. family   c. parents

1._____ a dad, mom, and kids; many things can change this unit such as divorce, illness, death, and older kids moving away to college or jobs.

2._____ nice people who fall in love, get married, have kids, and sometimes get divorced.

3._____ a change in the family which means the parents won't be married and live together.

Answers   1. b   2. c   3. a

Kids can't solve their parents' problems and they can't save their parents' marriage.

Divorce changes families. Your life is different now. List three ways your life is different now since the divorce of your parents.

       1.

       2.

       3.

Write down three ways your life has not changed since the divorce.

       1.

       2.

       3.

Kids are not the cause of the divorce and it is not their fault.

Divorce changes families. Draw a picture of your family before the divorce.

Divorce changes your family. Draw a picture of your family after the divorce.

Bad thoughts do not cause divorce.

Kids do <u>Not</u> cause divorce...
it is not YouR fault.

GREEN TREE
APARTMENTS

Divorce changes the family.

Doing something wrong doesn't cause a divorce.

Once parents get divorced, They usually don't get back together again. <u>Don't</u> hope for them to get back together.

Divorced parents very rarely reunite, remarry each other, and live together again.

Parents can take care of themselves.

Divorce means your parents won't be married to each other and won't be living together anymore. Draw a picture of the place where your father will be living after the divorce.

Kids can be happy living with one parent.

Draw a picture of the place where your mother will be living after the divorce.

Kids are taken care of even though their parents are divorced.

Matching (answers on next page)

a. clergy   b. cope   c. counselor

1._____ to learn to understand, handle, and live with problems.

2._____ priest, nun, rabbi, minister and other religious people, nice people.

3._____ a nice woman or man who listens and helps kids cope with problems, including divorce.

Answers   1. b   2. a   3. c

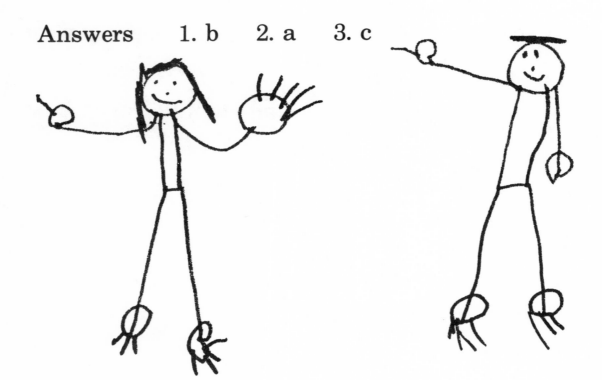

Parents who get divorced still love their kids.

Kids can give their parents a helping hand with odd jobs and chores around the house.

Matching (answers on next page)

a. work   b. sadness   c. psychologist

1._____ a nice person like a counselor; listens and helps kids and adults cope with problems.

2._____ feeling unhappy and upset; downcast; depressed. Disappointments often cause this feeling.

3._____ things kids do in school to help them learn; things parents do at their jobs to earn money.

Answers   1. c   2. b   3. a

Divorce sometimes means changing schools and making new friends.

Kids can live with one parent and it doesn't mean they are "taking sides" against the missing parent.

Write three ways you can let the parent who has moved away know you still love him/her.

        1.

        2.

        3.

List three ways you can help another kid whose parents are getting a divorce.

        1.

        2.

        3.

Divorce sometimes means living on less money.

There are usually advantages and disadvantages to every change in life, including the divorce of your parents. Write down two advantages of having divorced parents.

1.

2.

Just as a change has advantages, it also has disadvantages. List two disadvantages of having divorced parents.

1.

2.

Kids' grades in school will improve as they learn to share their feelings and accept the divorce.

Matching (answers on next page)

a. teachers   b. concentration   c. school

1. _____ to pay attention and direct your attention to one thing.

2. _____ nice people who work in schools and help kids learn many different things; nice people to talk with and share feelings and worries.

3. _____ a place to learn things and have fun while learning; has teachers, a principal, and kids.

Answers   1. b   2. a   3. c

You have learned many things about divorce and yourself. Write a short paragraph emphasizing one nice thing that you learned about divorce and yourself.

Divorce means taking one day at a time.

Frame I

Label each of the following statements as true (T) or false (F). Answers on next page.

_____ 1. Divorce ruins or destroys the family.

_____ 2. Kids can be happy living with one parent.

_____ 3. Divorce only happens to a few bad kids.

Answers for Frame I

1. False. Divorce **doesn't** ruin or destroy the family, it **changes** the family. Many things change the family such as illness, death, the birth of a child, and older kids moving away to college or a job.

2. True. Kids learn to adjust to **changes** in their families, which include divorce and living happily with one parent.

3. False. Just because a kid has divorced parents **doesn't** mean he or she is a bad person. Divorce happens to about **one million** nice kids each year.

Frame II

Is each of the following true or false? Answers on next page.

_____1. Kids can't solve their parents' problems and they can't save their parents' marriage.

_____2. When kids live with one parent it means they are "taking sides" and don't love the "missing" parent.

_____3. After the divorce the kids have to become "grown up" and take the place of the "missing" parent.

Answers for Frame II

1. True. Kids **can't** save their parents' marriage and **can't** solve their parents' problems. Divorce and marriage problems are adult problems the parents must face.

2. False. Kids can live with one parent and it **doesn't** mean they are taking sides against the "missing" parent. Kids can still love both parents.

3. False. Parents **can** take care of themselves and solve their own problems. However, kids can sometimes give their parents a helping hand with odd jobs and chores around the house.

Frame III

True or False? Answers on next page.

_____1. Problems, fears, and worries will "go away" if kids don't talk about them.

_____2. After the divorce there is a good chance the parents will reunite and remarry each other.

_____3. It is normal for kids facing a divorce to have many different feelings.

Answers for Frame III

1. False. It is better for a kid to **share** his feelings with his parent(s), teacher, grandparent, counselor, or a member of the clergy. A problem doesn't seem as big when it is shared and understood.

2. False. Divorce records show that divorced parents **very rarely** reunite, remarry each other, and live together again.

3. True. Kids facing a divorce often feel lonely, angry, sad, guilty, unhappy and confused. These feelings are all **normal** and **natural**. Sharing feelings helps kids feel better.

Frame IV

True or False? Answers on next page.

_____1. Kids are not the cause of the divorce.

_____2. Parents who get a divorce don't love their kids.

_____3. Kids are taken care of even though their parents are divorced.

Answers for Frame IV

1. True. Kids are **not** the cause of the divorce and it is **not** their fault. Parents get divorced because they are unhappy with each other and can't work out their problems.

2. False. Most parents who get a divorce do love their kids very much. Parents divorce each other but they **don't** divorce their kids.

3. True. Kids **are** taken care of even though their parents are divorced. After a divorce most kids live with their mothers, but some kids live with their fathers or a relative.

You didn't cause it.

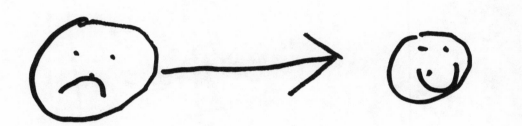

<u>Don't</u> blame yourself for the divorce.

I Live with mom and visit my
Dad on weekends.

All kids are taken care of after the divorce. Draw a picture of the place where you will live and include yourself with the adult you will live with.

It's normal and natural for kids facing divorce to have many different feelings.

Chapter 3

Learning to Cope - Sharing and Understanding Feelings

Everyone, including kids, sometimes feel tense and confused. These feelings are normal.

Matching. Place the letter of each word in front of its definition. Answers on next page.

a. embarrassment   b. confusion   c. anger

1. _____ a feeling of not understanding what's going on; feeling helpless; sometimes leads to anger.

2. _____ feeling extreme displeasure, feeling "mad"; kids often feel this way toward their parents after a divorce.

3. _____ feeling ashamed or less than others.

Answers   1. b   2. c   3. a

Everyone has feelings. Draw a
picture of a feeling.

Sometimes when I think of divorce I get angry and grumpy.

It is normal and O.K. to have many different feelings. Write down three feelings you had while your parents were getting a divorce.

1.

2.

3.

Talking to people and sharing feelings helps kids feel better. Name three people you can talk to when you have things on your mind.

1.

2.

3.

Sharing sadness and loneliness helps these feelings go away.

Matching (answers on next page)

a. disappointment　　　b. loneliness　　　c. cope

1. _____ feeling alone; feeling separated from family and friends.

2. _____ to learn to understand, handle, and live with problems.

3. _____ feeling sad or upset when things don't go as you hoped or expected they would.

Answers   1. b.   2. c   3. a

Matching (answers on next page)

a. fear   b. happy   c. guilt

1._____a feeling that bad things happened because of you or something you did.

2._____a feeling that comes when we don't understand or see what's going to happen next.

3._____a feeling of pleasure or joy; a feeling kids have when they know they can cope with problems.

Answers   1. c   2. a   3. b

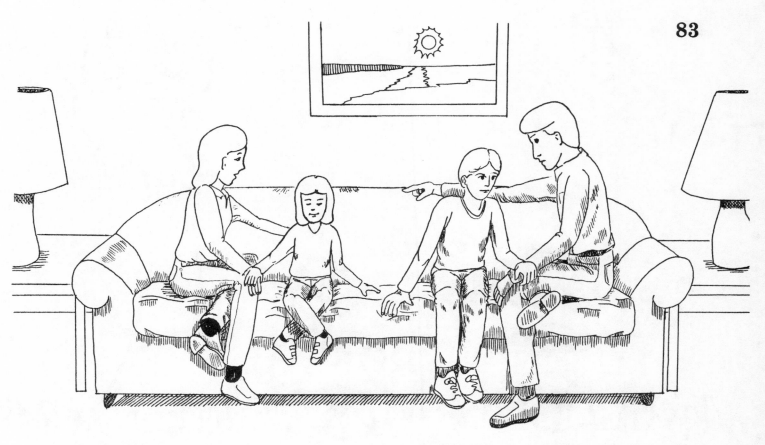

Fear of the unknown is normal. Don't be afraid to talk about your fears.

Sharing feelings and worries helps kids feel better.

I feel better when I share my feelings with my counselor.

When I cry I let my
sad feelings out.

Matching (answers on next page)

a. kids   b. nervous   c. worry

1._____young nice human beings.

2._____to think about a problem over and over again; it doesn't help solve the problem and it sometimes causes kids and adults to feel anxious and nervous.

3._____feeling confused, jumpy, and uneasy; tense; to feel as if "butterflies" are in your stomach.

Answers   1. a   2. c   3. b

It is normal for kids to become nervous or upset during the divorce. Sharing your feelings helps kids relax. Name three things you can do to help yourself relax.

     1.

     2.

     3.

When kids help others they also help themselves. Write three helpful things you can do each day for the adult you are living with.

     1.

     2.

     3.

Disappointment and anger are normal feelings kids have about divorce. It's O.K. to share these feelings.

Remember! It's O.K. to share problems and worries.

Grandparents help me understand.

Matching (answers on next page)

a. tension   b. love   c. shame

1._____ strong feelings of caring, affection, and tenderness.

2._____ strong feelings of regret and weakness; can be caused by guilt.

3._____ feeling uptight, nervous, and jumpy; confusion often causes it.

Answers   1. b   2. c   3. a

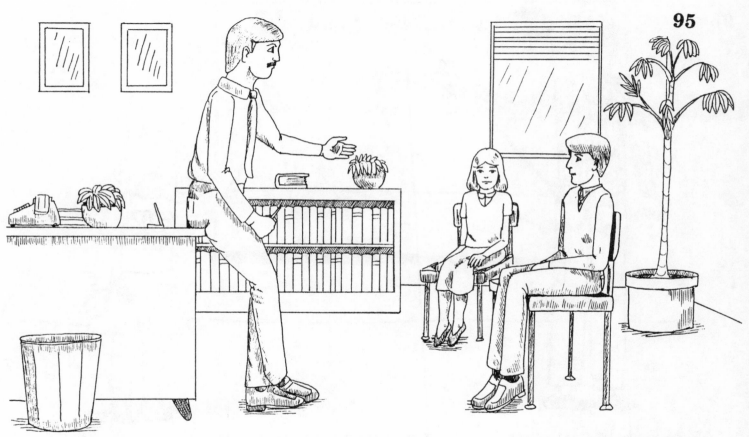

Sharing your worries with a counselor helps kids understand their problems.

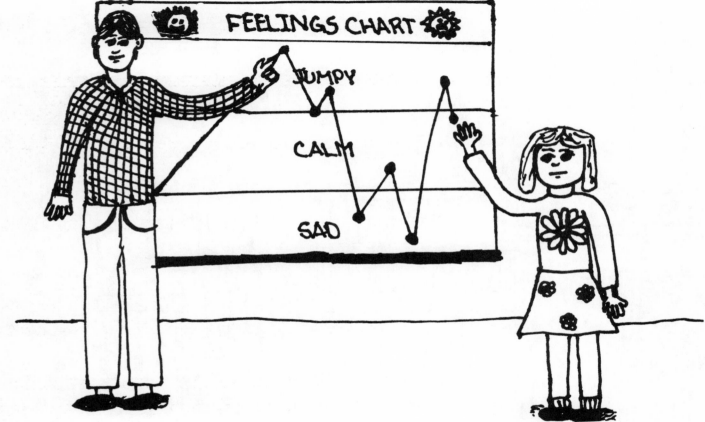

It is normal and natural for feelings to go way up and way down during the divorce.

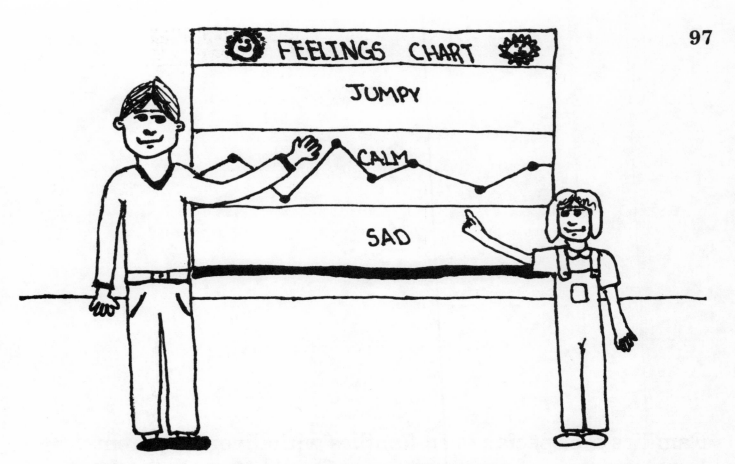

Kids calm down as they understand and accept the divorce.

Families are special; even families with divorced parents. Draw a picture of a person in your family you talk to when you have something on your mind.

Discussing your thoughts and fears with one or both of
your parents helps kids feel better.

Being organized helps kids relax and feel calm. You worry less when you know what you have to do. Write three things you do in the morning before school.

1.

2.

3.

Write down three things you do in the evenings after school. Now you are beginning to become organized.

1.

2.

3.

Teachers often help kids with problems and worries.

I Like to swim and it helps me feel Better.

Doing a kind deed or giving a helping hand often helps kids feel good. Draw a picture of yourself doing a kind deed.

Members of the clergy are people who care and listen to kids' problems.

Dear Mom,

Write a short note to your mom and tell her your feelings about the divorce.

Dear Dad,

Write a short note to your dad and tell him your feelings
about the divorce.

Divorce is sometimes confusing and scary....

.... but, as you share your feelings and worries ....

.... you can understand and cope with divorce.

DIVORCE HAPPENS TO THE NICEST KIDS - Revised: A Rational Self-Help Guide for Children (3-15), Parents and Counselors

Psychologist Michael S. Prokop explains divorce in a positive and reassuring manner as he concisely disproves fourteen irrational false beliefs concerning divorce that oftern cause children and adolescents to feel anxious, guilty, nervous and depressed.

After each false belief the "parent's section" discusses important recommendations for divorcing parents.

The book takes the reader, step-by-step, from "False Belief" to "True Statement" as it discusses such critical issues as causes of divorce, parental problems and remarriage, living with one parent, fears of abandonment, living on less money, academic regression, mood swings, support people, and more.

©1996 224 pages Bibliography Glossry 6"x9" Illustrated LC-85-72180
Softcover ISBN 0-933879-42-3 $14.95 Table of Contents CIP Program

"This extraordinary book provides children with honest explanations for the many difficult issues they find themselves experiencing throughout the process of divorce... may be used by members of the mental health profession, teachers, parents, and the clergy to facilitate the healing process and help children dispel false beliefs concerning divorce."

Cheryl A. Kendrick, M.S., The American Journal of Family Therapy, Vol. 18, No. 1

DIVORCE HAPPENS TO THE NICEST KIDS has received positive reviews in Psychology Today, Book News, Psychotherapy Book Review, Contemporary Psychology Journal, Curriculum Product Review, Marriage and Divorce Today, and Children and Teens Today.

DIVORCE HAPPENS TO THE NICEST KIDS, audio cassette tape.

The author reads the text and after each chapter discusses the concepts of the chapter with "Mike and Annie", two children who have experienced their parents' divorce. This tape also includes a "Kids Quiz" that helps kids further understand the concepts presented in the book. ISBN 0-933879-28-9 $9.95

KIDS' DIVORCE WORKBOOK

This workbook is designed to complement the text as it helps kids understand their parents' divorce and themselves. Helps kids feel better about themselves as they become more aware of their positive aspects and inner strengths. Successfully used by the author to help kids in group and individual counseling. ISBN 0-933879-42-3 $9.95 112 pages

HELPING CHILDREN AND ADOLESCENTS COPE WITH DIVORCE: A Guide for Counselors, Teachers, and Parents, audio cassette tape.

In this lecture, which has been presented on a national level, Michael S. Prokop, consulting psychologist, addresses divorce research findings, factors in children's and adolescents' positive and poor adjustments to divorce, and irrational false beliefs influencing their reactions to divorce. Offers numerous practical suggestions with case studies to illustrate each false belief. An excellent resource for your professional library. ISBN 0-933879-32-6 $9.95

THE DIVORCE GROUP COUNSELING PROGRAM

This unit includes everything necessary for a guidance counselor or psychologist to successfully conduct an eight week kids' divorce group. Helps children and adolescents feel good about themselves and they learn to share feelings, understand and accept divorce, and cope with stress.

Includes a "weekly outline" with processing questions, parent permission forms, participation certificates, eight copies of Divorce Happens to the Nicest Kids, eight copies of Kids' Divorce Workbook, one package of the PDAI, and one copy of each "divorce" audio cassette (4) described within. Successfully used in schools and clinics nationwide. ISBN 0-933879-34-2 $209.95 Save over $30.50

---

* The Divorce Group Counseling Program
is highly recommended in **Psychotherapy
Book Review** and **Psychology Today**!

CONCENTRATION, RELAXATION, AND COPING WITH TEST ANXIETY, audio cassette tape

This tape is designed to help improve students' test performance and they develop proper study habits, concentration skills, and test-taking methods. Helps improve confidence levels as it reduces test anxiety.
ISBN 0-933879-35-0 $9.95

KIDS' CONFIDENCE AND CREATIVITY KIT 8-1/2"x 11"

Written and designed by School Psychologist Michael S. Prokop along with a school counselor and three classroom teachers, this kit includes "35 black line masters" that may be reproduced and utilized by teachers and counselors to improve their students' confidence and creativity levels. Highly recommended for elementary and lower middle school students. ISBN 0-933879-33-4 $9.95

PROKOP DIVORCE ADJUSTMENT INVENTORY (PDAI) This four-page inventory is designed to help sounselors and psychologists diagnose children's and adolescents' irrational false beliefs concerning their parents' divorce. This easy -to-use instrument includes 54 incomplete sentences, 10 true/false, and a summary item.
ISBN 0-933879-30-X $10.40 (package of 20)

DIVORCE, CONFIDENCE, AND RELAXATION: A Guide for Kids, audio cassette tape (Prokop)

This tape is designed to help kids increase their confidence levels as they learn about divorce, stress reduction, and relaxation. Successfully used in group and individual counseling to help kids relax, disprove their irrational false beliefs, and accept and cope with their parents' divorce.
ISBN 0-933879-31-8 $9.95

WEIGHT REDUCTION THROUGH HYPNOSIS, audio cassette tape

This tape has been successfully used to help clients "choose" to lose weight by improving impulse control, confidence levels, eating habits, and body image. A must addition for a successful treatment program. ISBN 0-933879-36-9 $9.95

CONFIDENCE, PROGRESSIVE MUSCLE RELAXATION, AND AUTOGENICS audio cassette tape (Prokop)

This tape is designed to help clients focus on their positive aspects as they learn to cope with disturbing thoughts and stress. It also offers relaxation exercises that have been successfully used to help clients learn to relax, energize themselves, and enjoy life. Includes a "Morning Mind Exercise" and "Relaxing at the Beach".
ISBN 0-933879-29-6 $9.95

ORDER FORM

Alegra House, P.O. Box 1443-P, Warren, Ohio 44482, 330-372-2951

Please send me the following materials:

_____copies of **Divorce Happens to the Nicest Kids, A Self-Help Book for Kids** (Softcover)....................$14.95 each _____
_____copies of **Divorce Happens to the Nicest Kids**, audio cassette tape...$9.95 each _____
_____copies of **Kids' Divorce Workbook** ....$9.95 each _____
_____copies of **Helping Children and Adolescents Cope With Divorce**, audio cassette tape ....$14.95 each _____
_____packages of **Prokop Divorce Adjustment Inventory (PDAI)** (20 protocols per package) ....$10.40 each _____
_____units of **The Divorce Group Counseling Program**..$209.95 each _____
_____copies of **Divorce, Confidence, and Relaxation: A Guide for Kids**, audio cassette tape...................$9.95 each _____
_____copies of **Kids' Confidence and Creativity Kit** ....$ 9.95 each _____
_____copies of **Concentration, Relaxation, and Coping with Test Anxiety**, audio cassette tape...............$9.95 each _____
_____copies of **Weight Reduction through Hypnosis**...$9.95 each _____
_____copies of **Confidence, Progressive Muscle Relaxation, and Autogenics**...$9.95 each _____

SUBTOTAL _____

★*Satisfaction Guaranteed!*   Shipping: 10% of order; $3.50 minumum charge _____

Ohio Residents: Plese add 5.75% sales tax ....   _____
* I understand that I may return any item for a full refund within 120 days of purchase if not satisfied *
Name:_____
Address: _____Zip:_____

I am enclosing payment in the amount of : $_____.

I wish to pay by: ☐ Check   ☐ Money Order   ☐ Purchase Order # _____.